Introduction

"THE NAME'S BOND... JAMES BOND"

Not everyone's idea of a civil servant perhaps, but nevertheless our fictional hero worked for MI6 – part of the Civil Service.

Contrary to popular opinion, civil servants aren't boring people, doing boring work. The Civil Service comprises a wealth of interesting jobs! Civil servants such as customs officers, excise officers, tax inspectors, patent examiners etc. have jobs which are unique to the Civil Service. Others such as accountants, lawyers, librarians, clerks, secretaries, vets, engineers etc. have similar jobs to their counterparts outside the Civil Service.

The Civil Service exists to manage and administer government legislation and to carry out the policies of the party in power.

GOVERNMENT DEPARTMENTS AND AGENCIES

Government departments and agencies are generally organised on a functional basis: defence, trade and industry, employment, health, environment etc. As a rough guide, these departments and agencies can be divided into those that deal with: *Administration of the country, Government finances, Government businesses and services, the law, and people's welfare.*

There are over fifty Civil Service departments and it is impossible within the confines of this book to describe the work of all of them. However the following examples give an idea of the range of opportunities available.

ADMINISTRATION OF THE COUNTRY

There are a number of departments and agencies whose main task is administration of the country.

For example, the **Ministry of Defence (MOD)** administers the Armed Services. It is concerned with formulating and implementing defence policy. The Government receives help and advice from MOD headquarters' staff in London and both military and civilian personnel ensure defence policy is implemented. Service personnel are experts on military aspects while civilian personnel are the authorities on financial and political aspects.

The **Office of Population Censuses and Surveys (OPCS)** administers the law relating to civil marriages and the registration of births and deaths in England and Wales. The OPCS maintains records of all births, marriages and deaths in England and Wales and also deals with requests for correction to entries in registers, and applications for certificates. They prepare statistics on population, migration, births, marriages, deaths and diseases and, of course, carry out the regular population censuses.

LAW

There are departments and agencies concerned with the formulation, regulation and enforcement of Government legislation, and of administering the law courts.

For example, the **Home Office,** widely regarded as the 'law and order office', is concerned with the rules of our society, and how they are administered. The Home Office runs prisons, the police, immigration, and is also responsible for the administration of justice, criminal law, fire and emergency planning, firearms and drugs control.

The **Crown Prosecution Service (CPS)** is responsible for carrying out prosecutions on behalf of the police in England and Wales. With the exception of the most minor offences, it looks after over one million cases each year, ranging from traffic offences to treason and murder. The CPS reviews police evidence to decide if a case should proceed; it also conducts cases in the Magistrate's Court or will brief counsel if the case goes to the High Court.

GOVERNMENT FINANCES

Put simply, the Government *charges* the country for the services which it provides, and *pays out* grants, pensions and other benefits, to people and areas which need financial support.

Running a country is not unlike running a company. Both need money in order to pay their costs. In the case of Great Britain, the Chancellor of the Exchequer acts in the same way as a company's finance director and runs the country's finances.

The Board of Inland Revenue (see page 4) handles the collection of direct taxes and advises Treasury Ministers on policy issues.

HM Customs and Excise collects indirect taxes such as VAT, customs duty, and the excise duties on commodities like tobacco, perfume, alcohol etc. Many staff are uniformed and work at air and sea ports, forming the first line of defence against smugglers of revenue goods like spirits and tobacco, and prohibited items such as firearms, animals and drugs.

The Department of Social Security is responsible for all social security cash benefits, such as child allowance, housing benefit, income support, family credit and industrial injuries benefits. It also administers claims for

pensions and allowances for disablement or death while serving in the Armed Forces or in civil organisations during the Second World War.

GOVERNMENT BUSINESSES AND SERVICES

This is the area where the Government engages in business activities such as: transport, communications and energy, and services such as vehicle licensing and issuing of passports. The government regulates these industries and uses them as a means of income.

British exporters are assisted by the **Export Credit Guarantee Department.** This is essentially an insurance business run by the Government, set up to insure British businesses against non-payment by their overseas customers. Based in nine regional offices and two head offices in London and Cardiff, the staff handle the insurance of about £14 million of exported goods annually. A large proportion of the work consists of assessing the standing of foreign markets and overseas buyers. They also handle claims and provide back-up services in the fields of business promotion, finance and administration and international relations.

The Department of Transport (DTp) has some responsibility for the railways, bus services etc. It has direct responsibility for the construction and maintenance of motorways and major trunk roads in England (Scotland, Northern Ireland and Wales are looked after by their National offices), and also provides support to local authorities who deal with local road construction. DTp also deals with licensing, for both drivers and vehicles, road safety, marine safety, the coastguard service, and aviation accident investigation.

PEOPLE'S WELFARE

Throughout history, one of the primary functions of government has been to ensure the well-being of its subjects. Whether the form of government has been a feudal War Lord, or a full blown democracy, the principle applies; the government exists to look after the people as well as to 'run' the country. Most modern governments therefore involve themselves in schemes and procedures which provide for the poor and elderly, educate the young, and maintain a level of medical assistance.

Examples are the **Department of Health** which is responsible for administering the National Health Service. It is also responsible for the welfare services run by local authorities for old people, the blind, the deaf and others in need. It also deals with issues such as food hygiene and other aspects of public health.

Almost every aspect of education is dealt with by the **Department for Education (DfE),** from primary to further and higher education. The DfE is concerned with the training and supply of teachers and the organisation and inspection of schools. They are involved in the standards of design for buildings, special educational needs and also handle youth and adult services. The DfE implemented the Education Reform Act which introduced the new national curriculum and increased management delegation for schools. Most of the headquarters staff work in London, while statistics, computing services, and a few other areas are dealt with from Darlington.

THE WELSH OFFICE, SCOTTISH OFFICE AND NORTHERN IRELAND OFFICE

These offices are multi-functional, they adapt legislation and policies made in England to suit the needs of their own countries. They advise the Secretary of State for their country on developing policies relevant to that country. For instance, the Northern Ireland Office staff advises ministers on policies to increase security and stability and promote confidence in the future of the Province. Within each office are departments and agencies which are the counterparts of the main departments and agencies in the Civil Service such as: agriculture and fisheries, development, education, health, industry etc.

OTHER DEPARTMENTS

Not all civil service departments can be neatly fitted into this arbitary framework; some have responsibilities which do not obviously belong to any of the above divisions such as:

The Charity Commission which ensures that best use is made of charitible resources. It is responsible for deciding whether a body is a charity and it keeps a register of charities. It gives advice to trustees, and monitors and investigates charitable organisations as well as being involved in some investment activities for charities.

The Office of Fair Trading – Although British Law incorporates the principle of caveat emptor (let the buyer beware), the Government assumes some responsibility, through the Office of Fair Trading, for seeing that the public and businesses are protected against unfair practices. The Consumer Affairs Division looks out for unfair trading practices, takes action against offenders and sometimes recommends changes in the law. They can withdraw credit licences and obtain court orders to stop misleading advertisements. The Competition Policy Division (see page 10) keeps an eye on monopolies, mergers and practices that could be anti-competitive. Agreements between large companies to fix prices on a given commodity so that the public have no choice, can be stopped as can attempts to force shopkeepers to charge a fixed or 'recommended' retail price.

Many Government departments, nationalised industries and Commonwealth governments use the **Government Actuary's Department** as a consultancy service. This department advises on social security schemes, superannuation, pensions and insurance and other statistical studies.

This is just a brief description of the work of seventeen Civil Service departments. For further information on these and other departments, contact **Recruitment and Assessment Services** (address page 25).

STAFFING

Within each department of the Civil Service, there are a variety of different types of staff. Firstly, staff can be broken down into two types – administrative and specialist.

Administrative staff include for example, executive officers, administrative officers and people such as tax inspectors, customs and excise officers, Jobcentre staff and diplomatic service staff.

Specialist staff then break down further into three types:

Scientists – including meteorologists, vets, forensic scientists, chemists, biologists etc.

Technical staff – including engineers, architects, surveyors and similar professions.

Professional staff – including accountants, lawyers, economists, librarians, statisticians, museum staff and other non-technical professionals.

In addition there are support staff – secretaries, messengers, security staff, caterers, cleaners etc.

It is impossible to cover in detail the vast range of Civil Service careers available, so this book profiles just a few examples. It mainly concentrates on careers which are unique to the Civil Service, for instance, pollution inspector and patent examiner. However it includes three jobs – operational analyst, press officer and agricultural surveyor, which also exist outside the Civil Service. Professions such as accountant,lawyer etc, are covered by other 'Working in...' books.

TAXATION

Tax gathering is a career that has been with us for a very long time. In the ancient world, a number of taxes, including ones on imported goods, were levied in Greece and Rome, and Julius Caesar introduced a sales tax. Throughout history, taxes have also been imposed temporarily to raise money for wars. Income tax was first introduced in Britain in 1799 by William Pitt the Younger, although it had been in use in Italy since 1451 when it was introduced by Lorenzo de Medici.

Today's taxes are calculated and collected to pay for such things as defence, education, the police, the NHS and pensions. Two of the major Civil Service departments involved in this are Customs and Excise, who collect Value Added Tax (VAT) plus customs and excise duties, and the Inland Revenue who collect income tax.

The Inland Revenue calculate and collect the taxes due on people's income and business profits which include: income tax, capital gains tax, inheritance and corporation tax. The revenue is split into two branches – Taxes and Collection. Tax offices, which are further divided into PAYE (tax paid by employed people) and Schedule D (tax paid by the self-employed), calculate how much tax should be paid; collection offices receive the taxes, making sure they are paid on time.

CHRIS CRAPNELL

CHRIS CRAPNELL IS A REVENUE ASSISTANT (RA) IN A PAYE OFFICE

'As a Revenue Assistant I provide clerical support for the Revenue Officers (ROs). One of my first jobs of the day is getting out all the files the ROs are likely to need. During the day, I carry out different clerical tasks such as sorting the cheques sent in by taxpayers and passing them on to the appropiate RO. I list all the cheques and send them to the Collector of Taxes.

'Everyone has a P45 – a form made out by their employer when they leave a job. It says what pay they have earned and what their tax details are. When someone leaves their job we receive a copy of this form and I enter their details on the computer.

'A job I particularly enjoy is working in the tax enquiry centre because this involves meeting people. I take people's names, National Insurance numbers, tax reference numbers and ask them the nature of their enquiry. I then alert their RO, or whoever is appropriate to deal with their query. I also come into contact with the public when I stand in for the switchboard operator, and answer some of the more simple telephone queries.

'Many tasks I do are fairly routine but they don't last for more than an hour at a time. On the other hand there is really quite a lot of variety and it is a good way to learn about the work of the department.'

SHARON GREENSLADE IS A REVENUE OFFICER (RO), IN A PAYE OFFICE.

'I started my working life with the TSB but, unfortunately, along with my entire department I was made redundant. I applied for a job at the Inland Revenue, and because of my educational and working background, I was graded as an RO.'

As an RO, Sharon is responsible for the taxation of employees (known as customers) of a number of companies. She deals with the employees who earn under £50,000 a year, which includes some who pay tax at the higher rate of 40% and some on the basic rate of 25%. Although Sharon works in a PAYE office, she also deals with some people who pay tax under Schedule D in addition to their PAYE tax. A typical example could be a company accountant who also does some private consultancy work, or an architect who does some private design work.

'Most of my customers don't need to fill in tax return forms as these are usually only sent to people who pay tax at the higher rate or whose finances are more complicated. For instance, people who have a private pension or some kind of perks from work. If a customer does the same job year after year, we don't have much contact with them. Tax is usually only changed by the government; for instance, in the budget and the employer deals with this. Our only normal contact with people is when their tax situation changes, which could be for a number of reasons: they may buy a house and tax relief on their mortgage may not be handled through the MIRAS (Mortgage Interest Relief at Source) scheme, or they may get married. Apart from things like that, their employer pays their taxes and we just deal with any queries they may have. I have a caseload of 2,700 customers and I couldn't possibly deal directly with each person so it's just as well that this is rarely necessary.

'A typical day for me consists mainly of dealing with customers' letters and telephone calls, or seeing them at the tax enquiry centre. Customers generally contact me to ask my advice or to give me information.

'Typical enquiries are about whether they can claim tax relief, perhaps on some expenses such as trade union dues, or membership fees for a professional body. Or they might want to claim an allowance for a dependent such as a child or disabled parent. It's satisfying being able to help people; for example, some people don't realise that they don't have to pay tax on bank interest if it falls below a certain threshold.

'I receive a lot of letters. A customer may write to tell me that they have a company car, and I then have to find out all sorts of information such as the age of the car, it's engine size etc so that I can arrange for the correct tax to be deducted. Sometimes they might tell me that they have changed address or that they are going abroad to work. If an enquiry is complex, there are instruction manuals that I can refer to, or if it's really complex, I can then pass it on to a Revenue Executive. There is a lot of variety in my job. I never know what each day's post will bring in, and no two people's tax affairs are the same. I enjoy the personal contact both over the 'phone and at the tax enquiry centre.'

SHARON GREENSLADE

GARY WILLIAMS IS A REVENUE EXECUTIVE (RE)

Before joining the Inland Revenue, Gary spent three years working in an Unemployment Benefit Office.

'When I joined the Inland Revenue as an RO I spent four weeks at a training centre learning about aspects of taxation. I was then visited by trainers at work who covered specific subjects such as capital gains tax or independent taxation. During this first year I worked under a group manager and was responsible for dealing with employees earning under £50,000'.

Gary was then promoted to Revenue Executive and became a caseworker dealing with people earning over £50,000 a year – usually company directors (who may earn as much as half a million pounds a year).

'During that period, a large part of my work involved checking tax returns to make sure my customers were paying the right tax and that they were getting the allowances that they were entitled to. I ensured they were sent a tax return every year on which to state their income and outgoings. I checked these details against other information about their financial affairs. For example, I got a P60 form from their employers which told me what their last year's income was and exactly what tax had been deducted as well as what other perks they were receiving (company car, company pensions, free health insurance, etc). I also looked at information from sources such as banks and building societies who are required to tell the tax office how much interest the customer had received from savings, or paid on loans.

'Where tax had already been paid, I checked that it was the right amount.

'After completing checks, I issued a tax assessment, stating what their tax for the year should be. If I then found that the amount of tax the customer paid didn't match my assessment I would contact them to find out why. They may just have forgotten to tell the tax office about a change in their circumstances, or they may have forgotten to declare some private income from a spare-time job. In these cases we sometimes ask for an immediate payment to correct the situation, but if the amount is quite large we may spread it over a longer period, by increasing the customer's tax for the next year.

'The vast majority of people are honest which is why the tax system works, but sometimes we have reason to believe that a person (or a company), is trying to evade paying tax which is due. We do have Compliance Officers in each district who handle such cases, but sometimes I dealt with them myself. I may invite them in for an interview.

'Sometimes I dealt directly with a customer, sometimes with their accountant. I enjoyed dealing with the complex cases; it's very satisfying to sort out all the details and know that your customer is paying the correct taxes – no more, no less.'

Gary then became a group manager and this entails looking after six ROs who deal with tax affairs for employees of businesses in the centre of the city.

'My six ROs deal with the more routine tax work while I oversee and manage their work. I also organise on-the-job training for new entrants. I check letters, tax assessments and tax codes and I have to decide how my team are going to deal with incoming work. For instance, several thousand tax returns come in to us between May and October each year and I have to schedule a programme for dealing with them.

'The Inland Revenue is a good department to be in if you are ambitious because it's possible to get to the top quite quickly. I'm hoping eventually to move up to the position of Tax Inspector, of which there are two types; management inspectors who manage the office and technically trained inspectors who have been through an 18 month accounting and investigation course followed by an exam.

'I enjoy the mixture of figure work and people contact. It's not boring; taxation is a very complex subject and is constantly changing.'

GARY WILLIAMS

ADMINISTRATIVE STAFF
PROVIDING A SERVICE

A number of government departments and agencies exist to provide a service directly to the public, for instance, the DTI which offers help and advice to businesses, and the Employment Service which runs a national network of Jobcentres and Unemployment Benefit Offices. At present the local offices of the Employment Service are being merged into a single network of Jobcentres which will provide counselling and advice, job finding services and payment of benefit.

SUE DAVIS IS AN EXECUTIVE OFFICER (EO) IN A JOBCENTRE

Sue originally ran a day centre for adults with learning difficulties. But, unfortunately when funding was cut she lost her job. When she saw an advert for Jobcentre staff, she jumped at the chance.

'I started in a Jobcentre as an AO on the 'front line' – working at a desk in the front office dealing with customers as they come in. If they see a job on the vacancy board which appeals to them, we tell them more about the job and arrange an interview with the employer. We also answer queries about training, enterprise, grants and further education.

'My next job was as an Inner City Officer's (ICO) assistant. Inner City Officers assist clients who have been out of work for six months or more. Some of these clients were married women who were trying to return to work after having their children, and others were clients who had become demotivated through having been out of work so long. This type of work was much more informal than normal Jobcentre work, in that I went out to community centres to interview people. This way I was able to help people who wouldn't normally come into the Jobcentre for help.

'I had further promotion to Inner City Officer which is an EO grade. I ran the section; supervising my team and running surgeries to help the long term unemployed. I also spent time forging links with other people working in the same field such as careers officers and officers of the Department of Trade and Industry.'

Sue stayed in that job until spring this year when she became the team leader for the Jobcentre's front line team.

'I now have eleven staff and my job is much more managerial. It's very important to me that my team get job satisfaction so I identify areas for staff development, to stimulate and maintain their interest. Industrial visists are a popular way of achieving this and they provide the staff with vital information about working opportunities in our area. I also have to identify training needs and arrange for the relevant courses. I organise staff leave and ensure that there are always enough people to keep the front line running smoothly.

'I have introduced more in-depth careers/job interviewing to my front line team. Prior to this my officers were mainly placing people and answering queries. I also enjoy being involved in and helping with the interviewing and other front line activities.

'It's amazing how much job satisfaction there is in this career. I once had a client who had been unemployed for twelve years. Eventually after a lot of hard work, I managed to place him in a job which he was really happy with. It was a wonderful feeling of achievement – especially when he came back just to say thank you. Lots of our ex-customers send us cards after they've found a job – it's very rewarding.

'Another client the ICO team dealt with was on a degree course and wanted to become a residential social worker. We got him into voluntary social work and from there he moved into full time work in the voluntary sector. Now he is a resettlement development officer managing a hostel for young people and he now refers them to the ICO team for help.

'I'm really enjoying my staff management role; motivating my colleagues and seeing that they are enjoying their job.'

SUE DAVIS

THERESA KOLO IS AN ADMINISTRATIVE OFFICER (AO) IN A JOBCENTRE

After leaving school, Theresa studied full-time for a BA in Business Studies and then took the exams of the Institute of Purchasing and Supply. In 1987 she used her qualifications to get a job as an assistant manager with a large supermarket chain.

After having a baby, she decided to apply for some form of office based employment. She was taken on as an AO, on a casual basis, at a Jobcentre.

'After some introductory training, I was given an induction course which explained the role of the Jobcentre. I then went on to learn about race relations, conditions of employment, health and safety, interviewing techniques and how to deal with customers. I was given a permanent position 6 months later.

Her first job involved working on 'Restart'. This involved dealing with clients who had been unemployed for six months or more, discussing their future and offering them advice.

She also worked for a period on the 'front line' desk dealing with customers who called in to the Jobcentre for general advice or to select a vacancy from the board.

She moved on to work with a caseload of people who needed extra help, whether they were unemployed or working. They would make an appointment to see Theresa or another person on the team. Theresa explains:

'Some of them wanted to learn for instance, computer skills or office practice, and they needed advice on courses. Some needed help in filling in application forms, or wanted to talk about Employment Training. Others wanted careers counselling – perhaps a building company manager looking for an alternative career.

'Some of my clients needed help in applying for jobs. I might advise them which companies to approach and whether they should 'phone around or send speculative letters. I helped them with interview techniques and sometimes ran mock interviews to improve their chances.

'I also job hunt on my clients' behalf, matching their skills to vacancies. I ring local companies or write speculative letters. We have a good relationship with our local employers: we quite often screen interviewees for them and even do the preliminary interviews for them. As part of my work is to collect information about jobs and careers, I spend some time visiting employers to find out about their work. I also visit educational institutes like polytechnics to keep up-to-date with their courses.

'I consider that the main aim of my job is to help people into work, particularly the long term unemployed and disadvantaged clients. I really enjoy the way I see results from most of my work and I get great job satisfaction from helping clients and placing people in jobs.

ADMINISTRATIVE STAFF
WORKING ABROAD

There are a number of opportunities within the Civil Service to work abroad. Some departments such as the *Department of Trade and Industry (DTI)* and the *Ministry of Agriculture Fisheries and Food (MAFF)* have a role in the European Community. There is also a *European Fast Stream* which selects and prepares people for working in European institutions such as the *European Commission* in Brussels. Other departments such as the *Ministry of Defence (MOD)* and the *Diplomatic Service* offer staff opportunities to work in many places overseas.

THE DIPLOMATIC SERVICE

The role of Embassies and High Commissions (the name given to Embassies in Commonwealth countries) is to represent British interests abroad. The Diplomatic Service has almost 5,000 staff who carry out a variety of functions in Embassies, Consulates, High Commissions and international delegations in some 130 countries as well as in the Foreign and Commonwealth Office in London. Embassies are divided into sections: –

CAROL HINCHLEY IS A GRADE 7 DIPLOMATIC OFFICER

The Consular Section deals with people – either British nationals who live abroad or local people who want to visit or emigrate to Britain. They issue visas and assisting British tourists in trouble.

The Political Section monitors political developments in the country and keeps London advised of the situation. They study the local scene and visit outlying areas of the country. They discuss policy with London and then take the agreed action in the host country. This might involve for instance, negotiating a treaty or raising the case of a political prisoner.

The Information Section presents Britain and its policies positively to the local media and tries to get publicity for British businesses or cultural events.

The Commercial Section helps British businesses to sell their goods and services abroad. They give advice about local commercial conditions and regulations to British business people trying to enter the export market and help them make business contacts.

In addition there is **The Management Section** which looks after the mission (generic term for Embassies, Consulates and British High Commissions) and its staff. They manage the buildings and staff accommodation, and are responsible for transport, and locally engaged staff etc.

Foreign & Commonwealth Office

Originally Carol intended to be a dietician, but during her degree in nutrition and dietetics she realised this wasn't the career for her. She wanted a job with travel and decided to apply to the Diplomatic Service. She entered as a Grade 9, which is Executive Officer level and started work in the Foreign and Commonwealth Office in London.

'My first job abroad was with the British High Commission in Botswana as 3rd Secretary dealing with aid and information. We had a £6m aid programme which included some two hundred British people working for the Botswana Government in civil service jobs such as vets, planners, water engineers etc. They did specialist work and at the same time trained the local people to eventually replace them. They were paid a small salary by the Botswana Government and their pay was topped up by Britain.

'A large part of my job was the

administration of all these people. If they had work or personal problems they couldn't sort out themselves, they came to me. It was my job to help them or to put them in contact with people who could.

'When advisors came out from Britain and elsewhere to advise on the aid programme, they told me in advance what they wanted to achieve. I then arranged their itinerary making sure they met the relevant people and organised their travel and accommodation. I also had to arrange entertainment so that they could meet the local dignitaries and officials. In this job there's a lot of socialising because it's important for us to get to know the local people well. We attend cocktail parties, receptions, dinners etc.

'I was also closely involved with information work. I liaised with the local press, keeping them informed on various issues such as the British viewpoint on sanctions. I placed articles (sent to me by the Foreign Office or the Central Office of Information), with local papers and I wrote press releases publicising the aid programme. Prince Charles came on an official visit while I was there and so did Geoffrey Howe. I ensured that there were adequate facilities, including a press centre, and transport. I also accompanied foreign journalists during the visits.

'I really enjoyed Botswana; the job involved plenty of interest and a great deal of variety. I was a mixture of information gatherer, travel agent, personal assistant, hostess, press officer, welfare counsellor and general problem solver! I never knew what would happen next. I was on call 24 hours a day and had to be very adaptable.

After Botswana, Carol returned to England to learn Swedish at the Diplomatic Service Language School as her next job was based in Sweden. It isn't necessary to be a proven linguist to join the Diplomatic Service, but members of the Service have to be prepared to learn a language if necessary.

'In Sweden I was the 3rd Secretary in the Commercial section. My job was to help British businesses who wanted to export there. I also helped Swedish companies who wanted to import British goods, giving them advice and contacts. British companies needed advice on whether there was a market for their product in Sweden and how to market

them. They also needed advice on local taxes etc.

'Another part of my job was to gather general information about my commodity sectors which included clothing and food. I found out what was popular in the country, how their distribution systems worked, who the major stores and other buyers were and what the competition was. I then wrote reports on these sectors which British companies could obtain from the DTI. British companies also paid the DTI for me to carry out specific research on the market for their products.

'I also visited the large stores and retail chains and tried to persuade them to hold promotions of British goods – rather like a promotion of Dutch cheeses or German wines, say, in a British supermarket or store. (If stores agree to hold a promotion, Britain can sometimes provide financial help).'

Following this, Carol returned to England, to brush up on her French before going to the European Commission (EC) in Brussels on a training placement, to learn how the EC worked. She worked in external affairs and dealt with the relations between the EC, Finland and Switzerland (both members of European Free Trade Association (EFTA) but not the EC).

'I now work in the Foreign and Commonwealth Office in London as a Grade 7, (equivalent to Higher Executive Officer level) on personnel policy. I'm looking at areas where the policy could be improved – finding weaknesses in the system and making recommendations for the future. Part of our department is relocating to Milton Keynes so I'm also co-ordinating the personnel aspect; making sure that people know who's moving, when, and what allowances they'll get.

'I expect to be here for about three years then I'll be going overseas again; possibly to a political job this time. You need to be adaptable in this job; at any time you might have to move to a new job in a new country and speak a new language. This used to be difficult for married personnel, if their partner wanted a career too. It is still not easy, but today it's reassuring to know that there is policy of giving training grants to spouses to enable them to obtain the skills to be able to work wherever their wife/husband is posted.'

POLICY WORK

The main role of the Civil Service is to help formulate and implement government policies and each department and agency has staff involved in policy work. Their job is to advise the ministers in their department by working out the detail of how policies will work in practice and how they should be implemented.

For instance, in dealing with the problem of dangerous dogs, civil servants would have advised ministers of the various options such as muzzling, registering, or putting them down. They would have researched the facts, often consulting interested public organisations, drafted legal documents and discussed the practicalities of each option. Based on this advice, ministers would then have decided which policy to follow.

SAM SMITH IS A HIGHER EXECUTIVE OFFICER (D) AT THE DEPARTMENT OF TRADE AND INDUSTRY (DTI).

Sam studied for a degree in history and then worked in insurance for a short while, before he decided that this wasn't the career for him. He was interested in government and politics and decided to apply to the Civil Service to become an Executive Officer (EO) in the DTI.

'As I already had insurance experience I was put in the insurance division, where I was concerned with regulation of insurance companies to make sure that they were solvent. I had 30-40 small and medium sized companies in my caseload and I had to check that they had sufficient financial reserves to cover their claims without going bust. I was surprised to be given so much responsibility so early in my career, but there were plenty of experts around who could consult. The job involved visiting the companies as well as analysing figures from the companies which showed their outstanding claims and cash reserves. These figures were processed by a computer program which showed whether the company could meet future insurance claims for car accidents, fires etc, under various scenarios. The people I was dealing with were insurance professionals so I had to learn quickly!'

Two years later Sam moved to the Competition Policy Division, still at EO level. Sam's new division dealt with the regulation of mergers. For instance, if one bank wanted to take over another, the Competition Policy Division would help to advise ministers on whether it was in the public interest and whether it should be referred to the Monopolies and Mergers Commission (MMC) for further investigation. Sam's specific job involved the passage of a new Companies Act through Parliament, dealing with the legal framework for mergers.

'This was my first taste of briefing ministers and preparing their speeches. The opposition party has researchers to do this work, but the governing party uses the Civil Service. Working to a grade 7, my job to provide ministers with statistics and information to support their proposals and to demolish the opposition's arguments. For instance, if the Government wants to privatise an industry, the opposition may object or may make alternative suggestions. We would get one day's notice of the amendments being suggested, though we wouldn't know what their arguments were going to be. On the day, we considered the amendments, decided whether they had a good point or not, and then prepared the minister's brief, supplying them with all the facts they might need during the debate. If the amendments suggested were sensible, we would advise ministers to accept them.

'I also attended debates in the House of Commons; sitting near the minister, so I could pass notes if necessary. This can be very stressful work as you have to think very quickly indeed and there is no second chance if you get it wrong.'

Sam was then promoted to higher Executive Officer (HEO) in Research and Technology policy, dealing with EC funded research schemes. The EC provide large sums of money annually to help European businesses to research new products and to improve existing ones. A typical research project would be a more environmentally friendly car where all the components are recyclable.

'When I was promoted, my job involved researching what UK industry needed, and briefing the minister on what research programmes to support. Once the programmes were agreed by EC ministers I had to make sure UK companies had the opportunity to get their fair share of the available funds by producing booklets publicising what was available, how to apply for grants and what forms were required.

'When I first began I knew nothing about EC programmes, but I was soon explaining to UK business people how to apply for EC Funds and representing the UK's interests at meetings in Luxembourg.

'My next job involved dealing with the privatisation of the British Technology Group (BTG) – a small government organisation. I was second in command in a team of six. We had to get a Bill through Parliament empowering us to sell BTG. Again, part of my job was to brief ministers.

'Dealing with privatisation was a new area for me: previously I had never dealt with a sale bigger than a house or a second hand car; now I was handling deals involving millions of pounds! My role was to work with a team of people to decide the best way to sell – floating on stock exchange, a management buy out, a single buyer or a consortium of companies. We used city and financial advisors to help us and then I set out the pros and cons of each option, made recommendations to the ministers and then helped implement the sale.'

While Sam was in this job, he applied for the fast stream (see page 24), was successful and became on HEO (D). He now works in DTI's Air Task Force which aims to promote sales of UK companies manufacturing aircraft, aero-engines, helicopters and aviation equipment.

'My new job is in an exciting area – I'm off to the Farnborough Air Show next month to see some of the products for myself. I've found variety and interest in all the jobs I've had, and this is one of the things which has surprised me most about the Civil Service.

'You do have to be impartial in policy work – it wouldn't suit anyone who was fervently political because they'd have to work loyally for whatever party was in power. However, it is a job which gives a great deal of responsibility and it's good to see the results of your work.'

SAM SMITH

Within the Civil Service there are a number of departments whose role is to supply and publish information. COIC (Careers and Occupational Information Centre), for instance, which is part of the Employment Department Group publishes a range of careers literature – including this booklet. The Central Office of Information (COI) provide information and publicity services both at home and overseas for Government departments. Her Majesty's Stationery Office (HMSO) is the publisher for Parliament and the Government. It sells a wide range of publications in its own bookshops. Government Information Services (GIS) supplies press office and publicity services to central Government. They produce leaflets and posters, run national advertising campaigns and exhibitions and also produce their own publications. Their staff are employed in a wide range of Government departments.

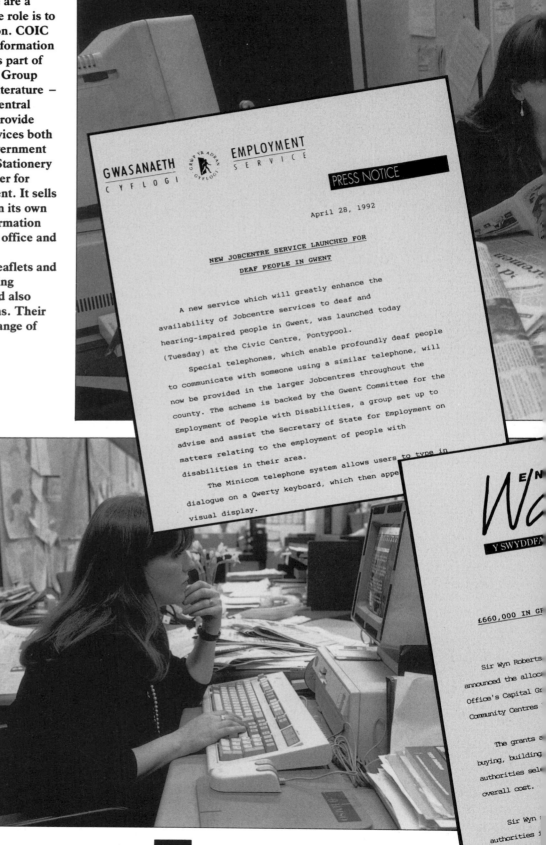

GWASANAETH
CYFLOGI

GRŴP YR ADRAN CYFLOGI

EMPLOYMENT
SERVICE

PRESS NOTICE

April 28, 1992

NEW JOBCENTRE SERVICE LAUNCHED FOR
DEAF PEOPLE IN GWENT

A new service which will greatly enhance the availability of Jobcentre services to deaf and hearing-impaired people in Gwent, was launched today (Tuesday) at the Civic Centre, Pontypool.

Special telephones, which enable profoundly deaf people to communicate with someone using a similar telephone, will now be provided in the larger Jobcentres throughout the county. The scheme is backed by the Gwent Committee for the Employment of People with Disabilities, a group set up to advise and assist the Secretary of State for Employment on matters relating to the employment of people with disabilities in their area.

The Minicom telephone system allows users to type in dialogue on a Qwerty keyboard, which then appe visual display.

E/N

W

Y SWYDDFA

£660,000 IN GR

Sir Wyn Roberts
announced the alloc
Office's Capital G
Community Centres

The grants a
buying, building
authorities sel
overall cost.

Sir Wyn
authorities i
this Program
the Welsh O
ble to app

NATALIE PEARSE

NATALIE PEARSE IS A PRESS OFFICER, WORKING FOR THE WELSH OFFICE.

Natalie left university with a degree in English and drama. She joined the GIS as an assistant information officer. Information officers may work in a press office or they may be involved in producing publications or work in advertising, exhibitions or even on radio or film productions.

'My first job was with the DTI publications, producing a weekly magazine called 'British Business'. I worked as the assistant to the news and features editor. In addition to on-the-job training, I was sent on a number of courses to learn news and feature writing. My job was varied and included the writing and commissioning of articles. Most of the articles were on subjects like exporting, franchising, customs and excise news, foreign markets etc. I was also responsible for copy editing, production and layout, so I got a good grounding in all aspects of publishing.

'Sometimes I was involved in exhibitions and had to set up and man the stalls and I did get a chance to go abroad to write about the state of markets in Holland.'

Natalie left the Civil Service for a while and went to work for Cable and Wireless, editing their staff newspaper. Then, after working for British Gas as a press officer, she applied to the Welsh Office for the job of press officer.

The Welsh Office is not quite like other Government departments , as Natalie explained:

'Central Government departments like the DSS, MAFF, the DTI, etc produce policies and legislation which, although applicable throughout the UK, are sometimes only applied in their original form in England. Wales, Scotland and Northern Ireland have their own offices which cover the equivalent areas of the central Government departments, and they may adjust legislation and policies to meet the specific needs of their different countries. The Welsh Office is divided into ten sections: Economic and Regional Policy Group, Industry Department, Agriculture Department, NHS Directorate, Housing, Health and Professional Group, Transport Planning, Water and Environment Group, Education Department and Central Services.

'A lot of my current job involves writing press releases. Some of them I adapt from press releases provided by departments such as DTI. For instance, they might send me information on industrial awards, and I adapt the story for the Welsh media, highlighting the Welsh award winners. I also provide original press releases on subjects applying only to Wales.

'I regularly have to deal with the press who ring up with questions such as: ''How much is the new by-pass really going to cost?'' or 'Is it true that the contractors are behind schedule?''

Press officers specialise in various areas. Natalie specialises in industrial announcements, and agriculture, economic and regional policy. She spends approximately 40 per cent of her time writing, 40 per cent on phone calls and 20 per cent out of the office accompanying ministers on public engagements for example.

'Our job is to arrange interviews for any of the press who request them and make a list of the questions they want to ask, for the minister. During royal visits we act on behalf of the Palace, not the Welsh Office. We find out what the royal route is, schedule it, and then work out the best places for the press to be. We notify them, issue press passes and on the day we keep them together and in one spot.

'Another part of my job is setting up press conferences. Recently there was an announcement of the launch of an anti-poisoning campaign in conjunction with the RSPB and conservation bodies. The aim of the campaign was to stop farmers putting down illegal poison baits for birds of prey – Wales was losing rare birds like the Red Kite. We organised the press conference for the minister, and arranged a demonstration of peregrine falcons and other birds of prey. We also ensured that the press were invited and were able to take the photographs they wanted.

'There are six press officers here and we take it in turn to be on-call during nights in case the press need to contact us. The morning after this we start work at 6.00am and go through all the morning papers, and get the news on radio and TV. Then we prepare a news summary for ministers and senior officials. This is one of the most tiring parts of the job, and answering phone calls from the press in the middle of the night is not much fun. But I really enjoy my job, it is extremely stimulating and diverse. I love working with current affairs and it can be exciting to be working at the centre of things, alongside Cabinet ministers.'

PROTECTING THE ENVIRONMENT

Caring for the environment has become an increasingly important issue over recent years, and within the Civil Service there are a number of departments whose work is concerned with environmental protection. For instance, *The Ministry of Agriculture, Fisheries and Food (MAFF)* and *The Agricultural Development and Advisory Service (ADAS)* work to prevent good agricultural land being lost. The *Department of the Environment, English Nature*, the *National Rivers Authority (NRA)* and *Her Majesty's Inspectorate of Pollution (HMIP)* have a particularly vital role. English Nature is concerned with the conservation of flora, fauna, geological and physiographical features and for establishing and maintaining national nature reserves. The NRA is responsible for controlling pollution and improving the quality of our river systems, lakes and coastal waters and their fish, flora and fauna (see Working in the Water Industry). HMIP with its increasing staff, now 309, is responsible for pollution control. It advises the Government, enforces legislation and carries out research into pollution control and radioactive waste disposal.

JEFF ORR IS A POLLUTION INSPECTOR WITH HER MAJESTY'S INSPECTORATE OF POLLUTION (HMIP), BASED IN BRISTOL.

It was while Jeff, a chemical engineer, was working with a large mineral extraction company as a development engineer that he became increasingly environmentally aware. He decided that he wanted to move into a job where he would be actively helping the environment. Around the same time HMIP advertised for a chemical engineer and Jeff applied. He joined them in March 1991, as an Assistant Pollution Inspector but because of his previous experience he was soon promoted to pollution Inspector.

'The bulk of my work involves carrying out site inspections of industries that have the most potential for causing chemical pollution, such as chemical and pharmaceutical companies, waste incineration, acid production, and asbestos processes. I also visit premises which use radioactive materials. A lot of my inspections are routine and are often arranged in advance with the company. However, there are many where I deliberately arrive unannounced. I might even arrive in the middle of the night, if I think I need to catch a particular company out!

'I usually contact the factory or site manager, though if it is a large company, I may deal with the environment or safety manager. I find out how well (or badly) the plant has been operating and whether there have been any problems that could affect the environment. I need to know about any incidents they have had, (such as emissions of a pollutant into the air or water) and plant failures. Most companies are now required to keep records of all pollutant emissions into water, air and land and I check these to make sure that they are within the authorised limits.

'The next stage is to look around the site, keeping my eyes open for any obvious indications of poor standards, such as emissions from chimneys, or any potential for pollution, and get a general feel about the 'housekeeping' of the site; for instance, is it kept neat and tidy? A well run site is less likely to have problems. I check that the operators know how to operate the plant properly, often checking their operating manuals. I also ask to see site procedures as these may contribute to the means of controlloing pollution and would include such things as staf training, control circuits, and management structures.

'The other type of inspection I carry out is the one following an incident which has led to the release of a pollutant into the environment. I often go with another inspector to investigate the incident. We take statements from all the operators and supervisors who were there at the time, and also get a report from the company management. The first priority is to talk to the company to make sure the problem doesn't occur again. Prosecution is considered at this stage if the law has been contravened.'

Jeff may then have to produce a prosecution report, talking to solicitors for legal advice. He may well be called as a witness. However, HMIP doesn't necessarily prosecute in every case.

'In the case of minor incidents or problems I tell the company what improvements are required. They let me know when they have completed any modifications and I then carry out a further inspection. If they don't take any action, I may issue a legal notice under the Environmental Protection Act, or other relevant act such as Health and Safety at Work Act, which will force them to take action. If they still fail to comply, the next step could well be prosecution. In rare cases I may consider that a site has a problem which could cause serious harm to the environment and in that case I have the power to issue a prohibition notice to shut the process down while the problem is dealt with.

'Although we are organised into teams under a Principal Pollution Inspector, each team member works largely on their own so we have to be very self-motivated and able to plan our own work. The workload is very heavy and we meet a lot of people, both operators and the public, during the course of site visits and incident investigations. It is a tremendously varied job; no two weeks are the same. There is a great feeling of achievement and satisfaction when I see the direct results of my work. For instance, if a site emits clouds of dust, I can persuade them to change their procedures and immediately see the difference. Some companies don't realise the harm they are doing, and they may actually think they are 'green'. If I can point out that they have potential problems, they are usually very keen to overcome them.'

GIVING GRANTS

The Civil Service collects money through duties and taxation, both direct and indirect, and it also pays out money in the form of grants, pensions, benefits etc. Departments such as DSS, Employment Service, MAFF and ADAS all pay out grants as part of their work.

THE AGRICULTURAL DEVELOPMENT AND ADVISORY SERVICE (ADAS)

This is an Executive Agency of the Ministry of Agriculture, Fisheries and Food and the Welsh Office. ADAS provides a consultancy service to all land-based industries. It advises an increasingly wide range of clients including companies and individuals and of course MAFF itself. To do this it employs amongst its 1730 professional staff a whole range of specialists – agriculturalists, horticulturalists, field engineers, landscape architects, architects, ecologists, biologists, meteorologists, soil scientists, microbiologists, nutrition chemists, mechanisation consultants, surveyors and many more.

IAN COWDROY IS AN AGRICULTURAL SURVEYOR WITH ADAS.

Ian always had an interest in agriculture; his father was a hop factor (grower's agent) and Ian spent all his school holidays on farms. On leaving school, he decided to study agricultural surveying at the College of Estate Management at Reading University. He joined ADAS in 1974.

Since joining ADAS, Ian has had a variety of different jobs, but throughout his career he has been regularly involved in two particular aspects of work; land use, and dealing with applications from farmers for grants. The role of ADAS has changed over the years especially since it became an Executive Agency and the emphasis of some jobs has changed. ADAS services are no longer given free of charge.

Ian first explained land use:

'In Britain, agricultural land falls into five grades. Grade 1 is the best arable land – you can grow almost anything on it, and grade 5 is the poorest quality – areas such as mountain slopes. Government policies are designed to protect the best agricultural land, to ensure that the country can continue to feed its population.

'When people make planning applications to change the use of agricultural land perhaps to a housing estate or for recreational purposes, the Local Planning Authority consult MAFF (or the Welsh Office in Wales) to see if they wish to object. MAFF then ask us to put in a report on that piece of land.

'As part of the Land Use team, I visit the applicant and discuss the proposals. I carry out a site inspection and have the land graded, which is done by taking soil samples for analysis. I also look at the farm and consider the effect of the planned development on the farm business. I try to get an overall impression of the part that the development site plays in the whole farm; it might be just a few acres, or involve all the land.

'I make a report to MAFF about the agricultural implications of the proposal. If the application is turned down and the landowner appeals, I may have to attend the planning inquiry as an expert witness.'

MAFF are also approached by local authorities for advice in designing Structure and Local Plans, ie development plans for the area; by English Nature for advice on the designation of Sites of Special Scientific Interest (SSSI's), and by other organisations who administer National Parks and nature reserves. Ian reads the plans, discusses policies with the relevant local authority or other officers, visits sites where necessary and then writes a report, again for MAFF.

Ian is also involved in ensuring that agricultural land used for purposes such as quarrying etc is returned to agriculture after the land has been worked.

'I am involved in proposals to extract sand, gravel and other minerals from the land. I visit the sites prior to extraction, during extraction and during restoration to advise the Mineral Planning Authorities on how best to restore the land for agriculture.'

The Government, through MAFF, offers a range of grants and subsidies for projects, many of which are concerned with pollution control and enhancing the environment. When a farmer has carried out some improvement work, they then apply for a grant. Ian's role is to discuss the claim with the farmer and inspect the work to certify that it has been completed to an approved standard. Work includes repairing old buildings − stone or timber barns etc − so that they can be reinstated as working farm buildings, new facilities to control farm waste and features to conserve the countryside. When Ian is satisfied, he reports back to MAFF who

then arrange for payment of the grant.

'I really enjoy the outdoor side of my work; I spend about two days a week out of the office. I meet a variety of people from farmers to planning officers and I have always enjoyed working in an agricultural environment. The only drawback of being a civil servant to me, is that I'm a cog in a machine, whereas in the private sector I might be running my own business.

'However, in my relatively short career, I've seen amazing changes in farming, from the production of food stuffs at any cost to a much greater sensitivity to the need to protect the environment. It is good to have been involved in that.'

PROJECT MANAGEMENT

As the Government is turning more and more to outside contractors to provide its products, project management is becoming an increasingly important job for civil servants. Project managers write the specifications for a job they want doing, whether that is manufacturing an aircraft or writing a 'Working in' booklet. They invite contractors to tender for the work and then select the appropriate contractor for the job. They oversee the contractors' work and help to overcome any problems they might have. The Defence Engineering Service is one of the many government departments which employs outside contractors.

DEFENCE ENGINEERING SERVICE (DES)

The DES is a part of the Ministry of Defence, employing a large number of professional electrical, electronic, mechanical and computer science engineers and naval architects. Its role is to ensure that the Armed Forces get the new equipment they need. The scope of work is vast and ranges from basic research into advanced electronic guidance systems and the development of remote control tanks, to the leadership of teams who procure multi-million pound equipment.

TECHNICAL STAFF

CAROLYN DAVIES IS A HIGHER PROFESSIONAL AND TECHNICAL OFFICER (HPTO) AND WORKS AS AN ENGINEER

After gaining A levels in maths, physics and chemistry, Carolyn wanted to do an applied degree and chose engineering. She went to Imperial College, London, to study for a degree in total technology which included languages and business management, in addition to engineering. One of the conditions of the course was that students should be sponsored. Carolyn considered a number of sponsorship schemes and decided on the DES partly because it was a large organisation offering a wide variety of experience for its students, and because it gave her the chance to gain a year's practical engineering experience before going to university.

'I spend my first nine months at a Student Engineer Training Centre (SETC). During the first ten weeks I learnt craft skills such as milling, turning and welding and some electronics. There were lectures and visits to manufacturers, and, throughout the whole year we had day release to college to learn about applied mechanics, electronics, control systems, thermodynamics and engineering materials.

'Following the basic training, we then worked in pairs on our first practical project. The remit was to design something which would be of use to a DIY enthusiast and would be commercially viable. My partner and I designed and made an electronic pop rivet gun. For my second project, I designed and made an electronic radio paging system. I finished off my first year's training by going to Fort Halstead in Kent to gain practical experience in the use of CAD in design and research.

'My next spell of practical experience came during my first summer holidays from university where I learnt about quality assurance. One of my jobs involved working on a new howitzer gun which was being made by outside contractors. My job involved working on the specifications for the gun. It gave me

some experience of working with contractors; they would often ring up to discuss any problems they had about the quality of the product. I also attended trials of the prototypes.

'During my second summer I moved into production engineering, through a placement in the private sector. I gained experience in dealing with production problems and I also worked on a project which looked at the way CFCs were being emitted into the atmosphere by a soldering process used by the company. I undertook research to find a more environmentally friendly alternative.

'After graduating I moved to Dorset to work on the maintenance and overhaul of tanks which were being refitted. My responsibility was for health and safety and I spend time looking at ways of improving the working environment. I then gained experience in estimating the time that would be needed for a refit (this information is vital for costing a particular job).

I had hoped to spend some time abroad during my training, so when an opportunity for a placement in Hong Kong arose, I jumped at it. I flew out there to work in a shipyard. My role was naval overseeing. In Hong Kong, they have three fast patrol boats which are used to prevent the smuggling of drugs, cars, illegal immigrants or arms. I controlled the regular refits and repairs of these boats. I had to ensure the work was done on time and was of the right quality. This involved regular inspections. I also looked at ways of minimising service costs.

'Working in Hong Kong was quite an experience. The first time I was taken out for a business lunch in a smart restaurant I was most surprised to be told to wear my working clothes as this is how people dressed. Going to a smart restaurant in overalls and boots is certainly different!

'At the end of my training I was regraded and am now a Higher Professional and Technical Officer (HPTO), working in London. I have just started my first job which will be concerned with project management of amphibious bridging. This is a joint project with the Germans and at present is going through the process of contractor selection. I am working on the specifications.

'Being sponsored may seem an easy option because you are paid during your training but, you really need to be committed, because working during the holidays after a hard year's study is not always easy. On the other hand you get such a wide range of training and experience. I got a lot of encouragement from the DES to take some responsibility for my own training and to arrange appropriate attachments for myself.

Sponsored Student/Graduate Engineer Scheme

The sponsored student scheme usually takes four years and consists of:

- A pre-university/polytechnic year of training including nine months practical engineering training at a Student Engineer Centre (SETC) followed by two months training at a DES establishment.

- Ten weeks work experience (including one week's paid holiday) at an MOD establishment during each summer holiday.

Final year sponsored students are invited to apply to the Graduate Scheme and receive eight further months training after which they are appointed to their first professional job.

After two years in this job they can apply to the Engineering Council for chartered engineer status and, when accepted, apply for selection as European Engineers (Eur. Eng)

During the year out and periods of work experience students are paid a salary. They receive £1200 annually whilst at university or polytechnic.

SCIENTISTS

INVENTIONS

THE PATENT OFFICE

There are over 16,000 scientists in the Civil Service, employed in a wide range of departments including the *Home Office, Department of the Environment, Department of Trade and Industry, Foreign and Commonwealth Office, Ministry of Agriculture, Fisheries and Food, Ministry of Defence,* the *Health and Safety Executive* and the *Patent Office.* Jobs range from investigating marine fish stocks to developing new weapons systems, providing forensic services to the police, and advising the Government on scientific issues.

The Patent Office, which is situated in Newport, Gwent, is an Executive Agency of the Department of Trade and Industry and is responsible for carrying out the provisions of the various Acts of Parliament relating to 'intellectual property', ie Patents, Trade Marks, Registered Designs and Copyright. They also advise the Government on policy in these areas. The patent system grants innovators a monopoly on the manufacture and sale of their patented invention, which may be either an article or a process.

NICKY CURTIS IS A PATENT EXAMINER

After studying for a degree in applied biology, Nicky joined the Civil Service as a research scientist. She then studied for a PhD in fungal genetics at Nottingham University. After deciding against going back to research, she answered an advertisement for specialists in biotechnology to work for the Patent Office.

'Within the Patent Office we have mechanical, electrical and chemical divisions. I'm in the chemical division specialising in biotechnology and I deal with patent applications for such inventions as synthetically produced proteins.

'Most of our applications are from companies although some come from private individuals. When I receive an application for a patent, it gives me details of the invention along with diagrams if necessary.

'A preliminary examination involves checking that the invention is described clearly and that it isn't a practical impossibility. I search through UK and foreign patent specifications, technical literature and databases to make sure that the invention is **novel.** I then decide whether it is **inventive** or just an obvious progression from an existing invention. I look for documents to verify these two points and then write to the applicant, or more often the patent agent who is acting for them, to tell them the results of the search.

'If they decide to continue the application I examine thoroughly all the documents relevant to the invention and make a judgement about whether it is both novel and inventive. Some of these cases are very subtle and require fine distinctions to be made. For instance, the mechanical division here at one time had to decide whether plastic shuttlecocks for badminton were inventive or an obvious adaptation of the earlier feathered ones!

NICKY CURTIS

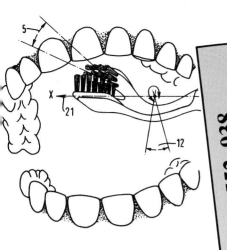

'I then decide whether or not the patent should be granted or whether there are objections. These objections are sent to the agent or inventor in the form of a report. The agent may wish to disagree with my objections or make amendments to the specification to remove the grounds for these. If they disagree, they have to convince me of their reasons. Usually this is all done by letter but we may talk personally to the inventor or their agent. If the agent and I fail to reach agreement on the application, both sides are presented to a senior officer in the Patent Office who has the right to make a legally enforceable decision. These decisions may be appealed through the courts, even up to the House of Lords.'

This work may sound simple but making these sorts of decisions requires extensive specialist knowledge, training and experience. New entrants spend up to two years working on patent applications under the supervision of a training officer before becoming fully fledged Patent Examiners. They also have formal lectures on patent law and are sent on French and German language courses as they occasionally have to translate applications. It is also a job for someone who is self-motivated, as Nicky explains:

'Although we work in teams headed by a Principal Patent Examiner, we work very much on our own; each examiner manages their own cases. It is important that any company or individual has their innovation or development protected, so it is also a very responsible job. What I like most about this work is that every case is different; I am making fresh judgements each day' – it's an intellectual challenge, and there is the great satisfaction of seeing a case through to completion.'

PATENT SPECIFICATION 1 552 938

1 552 938

(21) Application No. 27170/76   (22) Filed 30 Jun. 1976   (19)

(44) Complete Specification Published 19 Sep. 1979

(51) INT. CL.² A46B 9/04 13/02

(52) Index at Acceptance
A4K FX

(54) TOOTHBRUSHES

(71) We, KARL-HEINZ NORTH-EMANN, Ringstrasse 18, D-3501 Schauenburg 4, Germany and HEINRICH KRAHN, in D. Steinächern 5, D-3507 Baunatal 5, Germany, both citizens of the Federal Republic of Germany do hereby declare the invention, for which we pray that a patent may be granted to us, and the method by which it is to be performed, to be particularly described in and by the following statement:—

The present invention relates to toothbrushes of the kind having an opposed pair of bristle-bearing heads at one end (the "front" end) of an elongate handle. Said toothbrushes are referred to hereinafter as "double-headed toothbrushes of the kind referred to".

Double-headed toothbrushes of the kind referred to are known and have been described (see, for example, U.S. Patent Specification Nos. 2077392 and 3067447 and U.K. Patent Specification Nos. 366382, 482788 and 831.312). It is an object of this invention to improve on these known toothbrushes to facilitate powered operation by a mechanical or, especially, an electrical motor and to provide improved cleaning action on the teeth.

According to the present invention, there is provided a toothbrush having an opposed pair of bristle-bearing heads at one ("front") end of an elongate handle, wherein the said heads are mutually divergent in a direction transversely away from the handle, the free ends of the bristles of one of said heads diverging in said direction from the free ends of the bristles of the other head to form a longitudinally (with respect to the handle) extending wedge-shaped gap having in the said direction an acute included angle, and the handle is curved at its intermediate portion so that the longitudinal axis of the handle is aligned with the longitudinal axis of said wedge-

shaped gap to provide a common rotation.

The bristles can be arranged in bundles aligned in parallel rows to a square array and/or can be incline longitudinal axis and/or have th trimmed in a wedge-shaped man preferred that the bristles in the to of the present invention are arrang dle rows forming a rhombic ar arrangement has the advantage bundle can freely vibrate unimped acent bundles to accommodate tooth-thicknesses and intermedia

The bristles can extend perp from the respective heads or can to said heads, preferably to c wards the rotational axis of the It is also preferred that the uppe bristles at the wider-side of the the heads are bevelled.

The following is a descripti example only and with refe accompanying drawings (embodiments of the present the drawings:-

Figure 1 is a perspective vi headed toothbrush of one p diment of the present inven handle extension includin toothbrush oscillator;

Figure 2 is a plan view o of Figure 1;

Figure 3 is a longitudina view of the toothbrush of

Figure 4 is an enlarged brush head of the toothbr

Figure 5 is a cross-secti V of Figure 2;

Figure 6 is a cross-sect to Figure 5 of a modified

Figures 7a to 7f are toothbrush of Figure 1 i ner of use on incisors (Fi 7f) and on molars (Figu

SCIENTISTS

DEFENDING THE COUNTRY

DEFENCE OPERATIONAL ANALYSIS CENTRE (DOAC)

The role of the DOAC is to apply scientific methods to the analysis of important defence issues such as whether it is better to buy one type of equipment rather than another, what combination of forces are required for a particular type of warfare, and whether proposed reductions in the armed forces of different countries are likely to change the balance of power between them.

DOAC have for example, been comparing investment in future fighter aircraft to that of surface to air missiles. Recent studies have also compared investment in ships equipped with new helicopters (to improve the UK's anti-submarine capability) with expenditure on maritime patrol aircraft beyond Nimrod. Analysts use mathematical models and computers to help solve problems like these.

ALAN ROBINSON IS A GRADE 7 OPERATIONAL ANALYST WITH THE DOAC

Alan is the leader of one of the teams of operational analysts currently helping planners to cope with an uncertain future. In the present international turmoil it is by no means clear that the best replacement for an ageing tank or aircraft is another example of the same type. Future conflicts may require something quite different.

Another area of work concerns the balance to be struck in the allocation of

ALAN ROBINSON

resources between front-line fighting units and their logistical support: for example, spares, ammunition and transport.

Alan left university with a degree in mathematical chemistry and looked for a career where he could apply his mathematical knowledge. He had done some computing on his degree course and had played war games in his spare time. This, and his interest in tactics and strategy, steered him towards operational analysis.

'I entered as a Scientific Officer (equivalent to Executive Officer) and am now a Grade 7. My first job was as part of a team of three or four people, with a study leader and a military assistant. The team was presented with problems. An example would be – what sort of balance of forces and investment ought the army to have for different ways of combating opposing forces? For instance, do they need tanks, armoured helicopters, aircraft, weaponry, etc. and what balance is required? All of these attack in different ways: a tank can stay in one place if required, but a plane has to keep moving; however, a plane can fly quickly to a new problem area. For problems like this, we need some defence knowledge, but we do also have army experts to advise us.

'These problems are usually tackled in two stages. The first stage is to work through a set-piece battle. I work with two forces, each with a defence position. I input all the relevant information into the computer and play the battle through, changing the balance of the forces to see what happens. For example, what would be the effect if more planes were brought in, or what would happen if they didn't arrive? Or, if one force's technology isn't as good as the opposition's, would it go from a 'win' result to a 'lose' result, or would they just win less easily?

'The details of the forces; the types of tanks, etc. and the tactics are all flexible and I run the battle many times under different conditions and with different variables. You could play a game like this with dice and models and tables of results, but with a computer it is much faster and there are fewer chances of error.

'We have standard programs to use but I sometimes write changes into them to make them more appropriate for our particular use. We also have to input data

about all the weapons we are using.

'Part of the problem is getting the correct data into the computer. If a weapon exists and has been tested, there will be data available, but it can sometimes be difficult to get hold of. If there isn't any data, I have to persuade someone to try to get it for us.

'The second stage is to string a number of battles together and see the larger, overall picture. So, if in one battle we get a good or reasonable result by using the RAF, where should they be in the bigger structure?

The study leader looks at how it all fits together, interprets the total result and writes a report. These are passed to the MOD who use them in deciding what equipment and arms to purchase and other strategic decisions – such as the most cost effectiveness of our defences.

'I was promoted from Higher Scientific Officer, to Senior Scientific Officer, working mainly on analysis of the army and RAF support capability. Now, as a Grade 7, I am a study leader managing a small team. I allocate their work and give advice when it is needed. It is also my job to liaise with the MOD sponsors of our studies. I plan the study programme and interpret and present the results of my

team's work.

'During the Gulf War, I had to brief some senior MOD committees and I could see the results of some of my work, but it isn't usually so obvious. It's never a boring job and I love thinking through problems. You need to be a good lateral thinker; you start by making an intuitive leap which gives you an answer to a problem and it's only afterwards that logical analysis and the computer tell you that you were right.

'Sometimes we go out on exercises to observe the forces in action. It can be great fun to spend a couple of weeks living with them under operational conditions. We are there to monitor what they see, when they move, and how they operate and react. We piece together as much as possible about the battle. After abstract modelling, it's a chance to find out what the real thing is like.

The Civil Service recruits people ranging from school-leavers to graduates and people with professional qualifications.

Administrative posts

Recruitment for administrative posts is at four levels – Administrative Assistant (AA), Administrative Officer (AO), Executive Officer (EO) and Fast Stream.

Administrative Assistants (AA) and equivalent grades carry out routine clerical work such as filing, dealing with enquiries, simple figurework, basic letter writing and keeping records (sometimes on computer).

Administrative Officers (AO) and equivalent grades carry out a variety of jobs depending on their department. They handle incoming correspondence, write/draft letters, assess charges/grants, check accounts/maintain records (sometimes on computer) and assist the public.

Executive Officers (EO) and equivalent grades hold junior and middle management positions. They are responsible for applying the department's policy, ensuring that the job gets done effectively and dealing with the problems of people in all walks of life.

Fast Stream administrators and managers – this is a scheme for people who have the potential to rise to the most senior jobs in the Civil Service. Work could involve researching and analysing policy options, managing an operational unit or dealing with parliamentary business or operational matters affecting the day-to-day concerns of their department or agency. They could be consulting or negotiating with outside bodies; exercising financial management responsibilities or working in a Minister's Private Office.

Recruiting for AAs, AOs, EOs and equivalent grades is usually undertaken by individual departments. Fast Stream candidates and more senior grades are recruited by Recruitment and Assessment Services.

Departments such as Employment Service no longer require academic qualifications for entry as AA, AO or EO. Recruitment is via an application form which is designed to give applicants the chance to show their skills, followed by written tests in an Employment Service office, and an interview.

Precise requirements vary from department to department as do selection processes. However, a rough guide is:

AA or equivalent: 2 GCSE/S grades (A-C/1-3) including English language.

AO or equivalent: 5 GCSE/S grades (A-C/1-3) including English language.

EO or equivalent: 2 A-levels/3 H grades plus 3 GCSE grades (A-C)/2 S grades (1-3), including English Language, or BTEC/SCOTVEC National Award. Over half of EOs at present are graduates.

Fast Stream. The minimum entry requirement is a second class honours degree. Applicants take a one-day test and, if successful, they attend the Civil Service Selection Board for a rigorous two-day selection procedure.

Specialist posts

SCIENTISTS

The minimum entry requirements are:

Assistant Scientific Officer – 4 GCSEs/ S grades (A-C/1-3) including English Language and a science or maths subject,

Scientific Officer – a degree or HNC/D or equivalent.

Higher Scientific Officer – a degree or HNC/D or equivalent with experience.

Senior Scientific Officer – first or second class honours degree with substantial experience.

Fast Stream – minimum qualifications are at least a first or upper second class honours degree in a scientific, engineering, mathematical, computing or related degree. The selection process is similar to that of Fast Stream administrators and managers.

ENGINEERS

Minimum entry requirements are:

Technical Grade 2 – GCSE/SCEs grades (A-C/1-3) or equivalent.

Technical Grade 1 – BTEC/SCOTVEC National Award or equivalent with practical experience.

Trainee Incorporated Engineer – A degree or BTEC/SCOTVEC Higher National Award in an engineering or related subject.

Professional and Technical Officer (PTO) – BTEC/SCOTVEC National Award with relevant experience or BTEC/SCOTVEC Higher National Award in an engineering or related subject.

Graduate Trainee – An honours degree in an engineering or related subject.

Engineering Trainee (for the DES) – First or Upper second class honours degree in an engineering or related subject.

Higher Professional and Technical Officer (HPTO) – Honours degree in an engineering or related subject plus 2 years relevant experience, or BTEC/SCOTVEC Higher National Award plus 8 years experience.

Senior Professional and Technical Officer (SPTO) – To be registered with the Engineering Council as a chartered engineer and to have had substantial relevant experience.

Fast Stream – at least a first or upper second class honours degree in an engineering, mathematical, computing or related degree. The selection process is similar to that of fast stream administrators and managers.

Professional Posts – Lawyers, accountants, architects, surveyors and librarians are recruited as recent graduates and as mature graduates with a professional qualification. RAS also recruit fast stream economists and statisticians. Graduates wishing to train for professional qualifications may get financial help towards training.

SPONSORSHIP SCHEMES
There are a number of sponsorship schemes within the Civil Service for scientists and engineers such as the Defence Engineering Service (DES) student engineer scheme (see page 19), the Defence Science Group, DTI and Government Communications Headquarters (GCHQ).